CHILDREN'S
ATLAS
OF
SCOTLAND

REVISED EDITION

Theodore Rowland-Entwistle
and
Clare Oliver

Miles Kelly
PUBLISHING

First published in 2000 by
Miles Kelly Publishing Ltd
Bardfield Centre, Great Bardfield, Essex, CM7 4SL
This edition published in 2004

2 4 6 8 10 9 7 5

Editors: Stuart Cooper, Clare Oliver, Philip Steele
Designer: Sally Boothroyd
Project Manager: Kate Miles
Production: Estela Boulton
Cartography: Digital Wisdom

British Library Cataloguing-in-Publication Data
A catalogue record for this book is available from the British Library

ISBN 1-84236-363-8

Printed in China

MAP ICONS

Look out for the icons on the maps.
They show where there are special
features. They represent:

Airports

Castles

**Cathedrals
and Abbeys**

Forestry

**Leisure and
Pleasure**

Ports

Stately homes

Contents

Scotland

SCOTLAND IS THE NORTHERNMOST PART of the island of Great Britain, making up 34 percent of its total area. In addition to the mainland, Scotland has hundreds of offshore islands, which can be divided in three major groups: the Hebrides off the west coast, and the Orkney Islands and Shetland Islands to the north. Edinburgh is Scotland's capital city.

◀ **Scottish thistle**
In the 1400s James III of Scotland made the thistle his royal emblem. There is still an order of Scottish knights known as the Knights of the Thistle.

The earliest settlers arrived in Scotland about 8,000 years ago. When the Romans arrived in AD70, the inhabitants of Scotland living north of the river Clyde were mostly Picts, while British tribes lived in the border area. Later invaders were the Scots from Ireland, the Angles from Germany and the Vikings from Scandinavia.

Kenneth MacAlpin, a Scottish king, united Picts and Scots in AD843. The first person to rule the whole country was Malcolm II, who came to the throne in 1005. Throughout the Middle Ages there were wars between Scotland and England. Edward I of England tried to conquer Scotland in the 1300s, but eventually Robert the Bruce secured Scotland's independence in 1328. The Stewarts (later spelt 'Stuarts'), who were descended from Robert the Bruce's daughter Marjorie, ruled Scotland until 1714.

Scotland became linked to England when the Stuart king, James VI of Scotland, succeeded the English queen, Elizabeth I, in 1603. In 1707 an Act of Union formally joined the two countries.

▲ **River Tay**
The Tay, Scotland's longest river, flows into the Firth of Tay, an inlet on the east coast.

▲ **The Scottish Highlands**
One of Scotland's chief landmarks is Ben Nevis, Britain's highest mountain. It rises to a height of 1,343 metres.

▼ **Iron Age builders**
The Picts were warlike people who lived in northeastern Scotland. They lived in underground houses, known as weems, and built defensive round towers, known as brochs.

◀ **Patron saint of Scotland**
Andrew is Scotland's patron saint. He was one of Christ's disciples. Like Christ, Andrew was crucified, which is why his symbol is a cross.

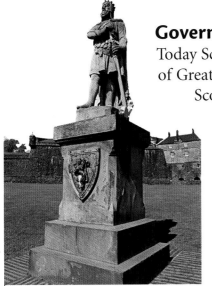

▲ Robert I of Scotland
Robert the Bruce was crowned king of Scotland in 1306. Almost at once he was on the run from the armies of Edward I, and later Edward II, of England. Robert finally defeated the English at Bannockburn in 1314.

Government of Scotland
Today Scotland is part of the United Kingdom of Great Britain and Northern Ireland. However, Scotland has its own legal, educational and local government systems. In 1999 the Scottish Parliament took control of many of Scotland's affairs for the first time in almost 300 years.

The Scottish Parliament
The Parliament, which consists of 129 MPs elected by the Scottish people, meets in Edinburgh. An executive consisting of a First Minister and other ministers is in charge. The Secretary of State for Scotland remains in the Cabinet of the UK government, and liaises with the First Minister. Foreign, defence, and economic matters are the responsibility of the Parliament at Westminster.

COUNTRY FACTS
SCOTLAND
Area: 78,789 sq km
Population: 5,054,800
Capital: Edinburgh
Major cities: Aberdeen, Dundee, Glasgow
Official languages: English, Scots Gaelic (Scots or Lallans is spoken by c.30 percent of the population, but does not have official status)
Main religions: Church of Scotland (Presbyterian), Scottish Episcopal Church, Roman Catholicism
Currency: Pound sterling (£)
Highest point: Ben Nevis (1,343 m)
Longest river: Tay (188 km)
Largest lake: Loch Lomond (60 sq km)

▼ James VI's family tree
The Scottish king, James VI, traced his ancestry back more than two centuries to heroic Robert the Bruce.

▼ Church of Scotland
In 1560 the Calvinist John Knox founded the Presbyterian Church of Scotland, which remains Scotland's established (official) Church. There is a statue of Knox in front of St Giles' Cathedral, Edinburgh, where he was dean.

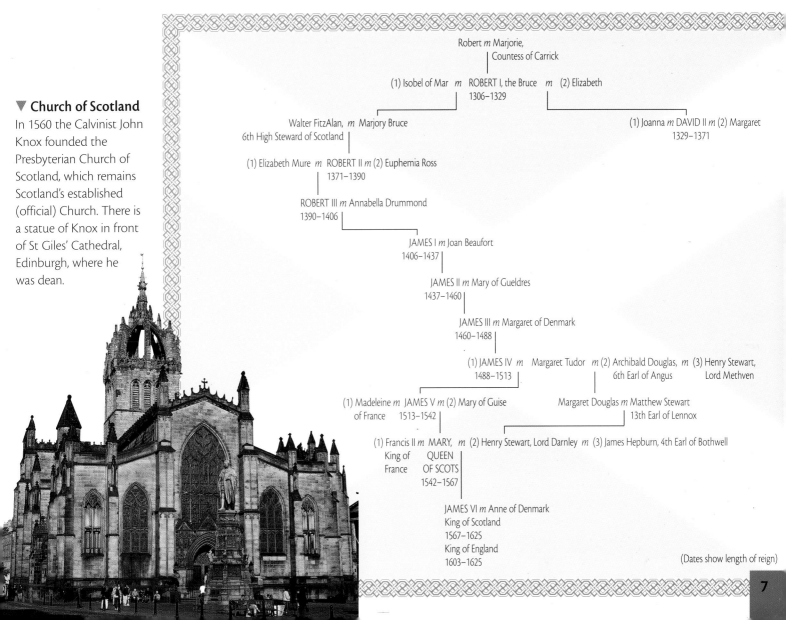

Robert *m* Marjorie, Countess of Carrick

(1) Isobel of Mar *m* ROBERT I, the Bruce *m* (2) Elizabeth
1306–1329

(1) Joanna *m* DAVID II *m* (2) Margaret
1329–1371

Walter FitzAlan, *m* Marjory Bruce
6th High Steward of Scotland

(1) Elizabeth Mure *m* ROBERT II *m* (2) Euphemia Ross
1371–1390

ROBERT III *m* Annabella Drummond
1390–1406

JAMES I *m* Joan Beaufort
1406–1437

JAMES II *m* Mary of Gueldres
1437–1460

JAMES III *m* Margaret of Denmark
1460–1488

(1) JAMES IV *m* Margaret Tudor *m* (2) Archibald Douglas, *m* (3) Henry Stewart,
1488–1513   6th Earl of Angus   Lord Methven

(1) Madeleine *m* JAMES V *m* (2) Mary of Guise
of France   1513–1542

Margaret Douglas *m* Matthew Stewart
13th Earl of Lennox

(1) Francis II *m* MARY, *m* (2) Henry Stewart, Lord Darnley *m* (3) James Hepburn, 4th Earl of Bothwell
King of   QUEEN
France   OF SCOTS
1542–1567

JAMES VI *m* Anne of Denmark
King of Scotland
1567–1625
King of England
1603–1625

(Dates show length of reign)

Scotland: Physical features

T HE GEOLOGY OF SCOTLAND IS DIFFERENT FROM THAT OF ENGLAND. Indeed, 400 million years ago, the two countries were on different continents. The two land masses collided, and it is possible to trace where they joined together deep under the border area of Scotland and England. Scotland's rugged mountains and scenery are the result of movements in the Earth's crust over millions of years.

Three geographical regions make up mainland Scotland. Bordering England are the Southern Uplands, which consist mostly of rolling moors with fertile soil. In the south, the Cheviot Hills form the border with England. Next come the Central Lowlands, through which three major rivers, the Clyde, the Forth and the Tay, flow. This area has the best farmland and mineral resources. The third region is the Highlands, which cover two-thirds of the country. This region is mountainous, with rugged peaks and numerous lakes, known as lochs. The most mountainous part is in the west. Most people in the Highland region live in the coastal lowlands, especially in the east.

▲ Mountain landscape
Scotland's mountains were shaped by glaciers, moving sheets of ice that covered the land during the last Ice Age.

▼ The Scottish 'Alps'
Winter snow on the Highland slopes provides good skiing opportunities at Aviemore.

▲ Loch Duich
Glaciers carved out hollows in the surface of the land. These have since filled with water to form the hundreds of lochs which are such a feature of the Highlands.

1
2
3
4

◄ Shifting lands
Once separated by sea, Scotland and England were pushed together as a result of continental drift. This was the movement of the Earth's land masses that took place over a period of millions of years:
1 Around 280 million years ago (mya), the land formed one giant supercontinent, Pangaea
2 Around 180 mya, Pangaea split into Laurasia (to the north) and Gondwanaland (to the south)
3 Around 65 mya, the Atlantic Ocean widened
4 Today, the land masses are grouped into seven continents

◄ Stormy seas
The rocky Grampian coast takes a regular battering from the North Sea waves.

CLIMATE
Scotland's climate is mainly mild, but it is cooler and wetter than the climate of England and Wales. The prevailing winds come from the southwest. They bring a series of weather fronts across the island. Scotland, like Wales, parts of western England and northern Ireland, receives more rain than eastern England. Rainfall is lower along Scotland's east coast because of the so-called 'rain shadow' cast by the mountains. The average annual rainfall in Edinburgh is 750–1,000 mm, while in the west of Scotland it is more than 1,500 mm. During the winter months, snow falls in the Highlands.

ATLANTIC OCEAN

NORTH SEA

◄ Highs and lows
The Scottish Lowlands are the best region for arable farming. In the Highlands, farmers raise sheep and hardy, long-coated Highland Cattle.

▲ Firth of Forth
The river Forth, with its long estuary, or firth, marks the dividing line between the Highlands and the rest of Scotland.

Moving mountains

When the Atlantic Ocean began to open up about sixty-five million years ago, the land which is now Scotland remained joined to what is now Europe. The rest of that continent formed what is now North America. The hard rocks that make up Scotland's mountains were crushed, folded and distorted many times – and even turned upside down! Originally the mountains were sharp and jagged. Millions of years of action by wind, rain and ice have worn them down, so they are much lower than their original height with rounded outlines.

The Great Glen

Glen Mor, or the Great Glen, is the remains of a huge geological fault in the Earth's crust. It may once have been similar to the earthquake-prone San Andreas Fault in California, where two of the Earth's plates are grating against one another.

Edinburgh

◄ Loyal landmark
Bobby the Skye terrier waited loyally for his dead master in the same spot for 14 years. There is a statue of him in front of Greyfriar's Kirk.

EDINBURGH HAS BEEN THE CAPITAL OF SCOTLAND since the beginning of the 15th century, when it replaced the Scottish capital of Perth. In 1999 it became the seat of the revived Scottish Parliament. Built around the banks of the Forth Estuary, Edinburgh is ideally sited in the Central Lowlands, a region of rich farmland and extensive mineral deposits.

▲ Unfinished business
Funds to build the Greek-style National Monument, atop Calton Hill, ran out after just 12 columns were complete.

Edinburgh has direct rail and road links with London, and air services link it with United Kingdom cities and several capital cities in continental Europe. Rail and road bridges span the Firth of Forth to link the city with the northern part of the country. There are many different industries in and around the capital, including brewing, whisky distilling, and textile and paper manufacturing. Edinburgh is also a key business centre, with many banks and insurance offices.

▲ Street juggler
The Edinburgh International Festival attracts hoards of tourists to the city each August. Performers include actors, comedians and street entertainers.

Important buildings

The magnificent castle, perched high up on its rocky crag, dominates the city. It stands on the plug of a long-dead volcano. To the north of the castle rock is a valley through which the railway line runs, and on the far side is Princes Street, one of the main shopping centres. Nearby is Calton Hill, another volcanic plug, which is topped by the Nelson Monument. To the east of the city is the magnificent hill of Arthur's Seat, set in Holyrood Park. On the edge of the park stands the Palace of Holyroodhouse. Several Scottish kings and queens are buried in the palace's vault. Other notable buildings include St Giles' Cathedral, the Royal Observatory on Calton Hill, and Register House.

▼ Royal guesthouse
The Palace of Holyroodhouse is the Queen's official residence in Scotland.

▼ Museum of Scotland
Opened in 1998, the new Museum of Scotland houses a collection of artefacts from Scottish history.

The oldest of the city's three universities was founded in 1583. Edinburgh also has two famous medical colleges: the Royal College of Physicians of Edinburgh and the Royal College of Surgeons of Edinburgh. The Meadowbank Sports Centre hosted the 1970 Commonwealth Games.

Moments in history

There has been a settlement at Edinburgh since 850BC. Edinburgh grew in the AD1000s when David I established his court at Edinburgh Castle. In 1513 the English defeated the Scots at the Battle of Flodden, killing James IV and 10,000 of his men. Afterwards the Scots built new defences around Edinburgh. Remains of 'Flodden Wall' can still be seen on the High Street. When James VI became King of England in 1603, the royal court moved to London. In the 1700s many new buildings were erected to the north of the old city. In the 1800s the population of the city quadrupled, and many terraced houses were built. Today, the city has a population of 420,170.

▲ **Edinburgh streets**
Many of Edinburgh's buildings date back to the 1700s. The 37-km-long Water of Leith meanders through the city.

◀ **Regimental entertainment**
Against the impressive backdrop of the castle, Edinburgh's Military Tattoo is held at the end of August each year, to coincide with the Edinburgh Festival.

◀ **Wall plaque, the Royal Mile**
Leading up to Edinburgh Castle, the Royal Mile is lined with beautiful buildings, some dating to the 1400s.

▲ **Seat of learning**
Graduates of Edinburgh University have included Charles Darwin, writers Thomas Carlyle and Sir Walter Scott, and the inventor Alexander Graham Bell.

West to Galloway

▼ Religious ruins
Sweetheart Abbey, near Kirkcudbright, was a centre for Cistercian monks from 1273 until 1603.

▼ Poem in stone
Ruthwell Cross dates from the AD700s. It is covered with ancient runes, or writing. The inscription includes part of an Old English poem called *The Dream of the Rood*, which is about Christ's crucifixion.

THE DUMFRIES AND GALLOWAY REGION lies in southwestern Scotland. It contains the former counties of Dumfriesshire, Kirkcudbrightshire and Wigtownshire. Ireland is only 21 kilometres away across a stretch of water called the North Channel.

Most of this region is low-lying coastal land, broken up by rocky headlands. To the north lies a plateau of moorland. In the west is a hammer-head shaped peninsula called the Rhins of Galloway. It stretches south to the Mull of Galloway, a towering 64-metre-high cliff. In the northern part of the Rhins is the port of Stranraer, which runs a regular shipping service to Larne in Northern Ireland.

◀ Rose-tinted fortress
Caerlaverock Castle has stood on the shores of the Solway Firth since the 1290s.

Farming and industry

Farmers in Dumfries and Galloway rear sheep, cattle and pigs, and grow oats, turnips and other cattle feed. Potatoes are the main crop grown for human consumption. There are five hydroelectric power stations in Kirkcudbrightshire, which use water from local rivers and lochs to generate electricity. Wigtown is being developed as the centre of Scotland's book trade. Tourism is important in the region. Kirkcudbright attracts artists and anglers. The fishing is also good at Gatehouse of Fleet on the river Fleet.

▲ Barnacle goose

GRETNA GREEN
Close to the border with England lies the village of Gretna Green. For centuries English couples ran away and married here. Under Scots law, under-age brides did not need their parents' permission to marry.

◀ Salmon leap
Scotland is famous for its freshwater fish. Wild salmon head upriver each year to their spawning grounds.

▶ Power station
This hydroelectric dam harnesses water power. The energy of water driving a turbine is changed into electrical energy at the power station.

Moments in history

People have lived in this region since around 5000BC. The Stone Age tombs at Cairnholy, near Gatehouse of Fleet, date from about 3000BC. At Burnswark, near Lockerbie, you can see the remains of an Iron Age hill fort and two Roman camps. St Ninian, who founded a monastery at Whithorn, near Burrow Head, is said to have brought Christianity to the area in about AD390. Later, Viking invaders from Scandinavia and Normans from England occupied the area. Dumfriesshire became a Scottish shire, or county, in the 1400s.

▲ Viking invaders

LOCAL GOVERNMENT

UNITARY COUNCIL
Dumfries and Galloway
Note: pages 122–23 explain the different types of local authority and show the areas covered by the bodies in this region.

F

E

D

C

B

A

Moffat

Nith

Annan

SOUTHERN UPLANDS

Lockerbie

Dumfries

Sweetheart Abbey

Caerlaverock Castle

Gretna Green

Castle Douglas

Dalbeattie

Solway Firth

Dee

Galloway Forest Park

Newton Stewart

NORTH CHANNEL

Rhins of Galloway

Stranraer

Wigtown

Gatehouse of Fleet

Wigtown Bay

Kirkudbright Castle

Kirkcudbright

Luce Bay

IRISH SEA

Burrow Head

Mull of Galloway

◀ **Grim and grey**
Now in ruins, Threave Castle on the river Dee was the home of a fierce clan, the Black Douglases. The earls of Douglas found a grisly use for the post that sticks out above the castle doorway. This was where they hung 'tassels' – that is, their poor enemies!

ROBBIE'S HOUSE
Robert Burns was one of Scotland's greatest poets. He spent the last five years of his life in Dumfries, where he worked as a tax collector. He described the town as 'Maggie by the Banks o' Nith.' His house is now a museum.

The Scottish Borders

▼ Melrose Abbey
These Gothic ruins near Galashiels were restored by Sir Walter Scott in the 1800s. Robert the Bruce's heart is buried here.

THE SCOTTISH BORDER REGIONS HAVE A LONG FRONTIER with England, sloping from southwest to northeast. Much of the land on either side of the border is wild country, with steep hills, fast-flowing streams and few towns or villages. The Border regions include the former counties of Berwickshire, Peeblesshire, Roxburghshire and Selkirkshire.

▼ Order of the Garter
Coldstream, on the banks of the river Tweed, was the birthplace of the British Army's oldest regiment, the Coldstream Guards. The regiment's emblem is the Star of the Order of the Garter.

Most of the land in the Scottish Borders forms part of the Southern Uplands. These eroded, rounded hills are covered with grass and heather. They include the Cheviots along the English border – the highest peak is The Cheviot (816 metres). To the north are the Pentland, Moorfoot and Lammermuir Hills. In the east is a lowland area called the Merse, a rich farming region. The river Tweed, with its many tributaries, flows between the hills and through the fertile Merse to the sea. The region has warm summers and cold winters. Its rainfall is very variable, ranging from 625 to 1,750 mm per year.

Farming and industry

About half of the land in the Borders is used for grazing sheep and cattle. Farmers grow barley, wheat and potatoes, and grass, turnips and other crops for animal feed. Ettrick Forest is the remains of a huge ancient forest, and there are modern plantations of pine. Foxes, badgers and rabbits are common, and roe-deer live in some of the forests. Salmon breed in the river Tweed. There is a small amount of industry, largely textiles, with tweed cloth as the main output. Jedburgh is a centre of the tweed industry.

◄ Boats of Berwickshire
Eyemouth is the region's chief fishing harbour.

◄ Scots pine

▶ Rabbit

▶ River Tweed

Moments in history

The Borders were part of the English kingdom of Northumbria until AD876, when Northumbria ceased to exist as a separate kingdom. The Borders were then part of England until the early 1000s, when the region was taken into Scotland. An exception was the town of Berwick-upon-Tweed, which changed hands between England and Scotland several times before finally becoming part of England in 1482. At the same time, powerful Scottish families, such as the Douglases, competed with one another for power. Greenknowe Tower, near Earlston, was built as a stronghold in 1581, when border skirmishes were still common.

▲ **Wild reivers**
From the 1200s to the 1500s the whole area of the Borders was ravaged by wars, skirmishes and reiving (plundering).

NORTH SEA

Eyemouth

Duns

Tweed

Coldstream

Kelso

MOORFOOT HILLS
▲ *Blackhope Scar*

Peebles
Tweed

Abbotsford
Melrose Abbey
Galashiels
Melrose

Roxburgh

Selkirk
Teviot
Jedburgh

Ettrick Forest
Ettrick
Hawick

CHEVIOT HILLS

LOCAL GOVERNMENT

UNITARY COUNCIL
Scottish Borders

Note: pages 122–23 explain the different types of local authority and show the areas covered by the bodies in this region.

▲ **Romantic house**
Abbotsford is a large house near Melrose. It was built by the novelist and poet Sir Walter Scott, who wrote his 30 'Waverley novels' there. These were romantic tales of knights and ladies, set in the Scottish Borders.

▶ **Duns Scotus**

WHAT'S IN A NAME?
The Franciscan priest and philosopher Duns Scotus was born at Duns in Berwickshire in 1265. The word 'dunce' comes from his name, because his followers were supposed to be against learning.

F

E

D

C

B

A

Lothian

▼ Firth of Forth

THE LOTHIAN REGION IS DIVIDED INTO THREE PARTS: West Lothian, Midlothian and East Lothian. The region makes up only about two percent of Scotland's total area, but almost 30 percent of the country's population live there, mostly in the city of Edinburgh.

Lothian, which forms part of the Central Lowlands of Scotland, is bordered by moorland hills. To the southwest are the Pentland Hills, the highest part of which is Scald Law (580 metres). To the southeast are the Moorfoot and Lammermuir Hills, many of which are long-extinct volcanoes. The highest point is Blackhope Scar (650 metres). Four main rivers drain the region – the Almond, the Tyne, the Esk and the Water of Leith.

Towns, transport and industry

Two huge bridges near Edinburgh, the Forth Rail Bridge and the Forth Road Bridge, link Lothian with the north bank of the River Forth. Besides Edinburgh, the region's largest towns are Livingston, Musselburgh, Bathgate, Whitburn, Penicuick and Dalkeith. In 1962 Livingston was a village with a population of only 2,000. It was designated as a 'new town' in that year, and by 1991 it had over 41,000 inhabitants. There are firms producing electronics and other technological products at Dalkeith and Livingston, but most of the region's industry is concentrated in Edinburgh.

▲ Seaweed

▼ **Pigeon castle**
Lothian has several doocots, or dovecots, where people bred rock doves (pigeons) for eggs and meat. This doocot at West Saltoun looks like a miniature, turreted castle!

▼ **Bass Rock**
Just off the coast of East Lothian, this 107-metre-high rock is the plug of a long-extinct volcano.

▼ **Circuit board**
There are electronics companies in and around Dalkeith.

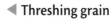
◀ **Threshing grain**
Andrew Meikle was a millwright at Houston Mill, near Dunbar. In 1788 he patented a brand-new threshing machine that removed wheat and grain from their husks, or chaff.

Farming and wildlife

Arable farming and market gardening are extensive in Lothian. Farmers raise sheep in the Lammermuir Hills, as well as cattle and chickens. Seabird colonies thrive on the Bass Rock, North Berwick Law and other islands in the Firth of Forth, and in a reserve at Aberlady Bay. The Isle of May, in the mouth of the Firth, is used as a stopover by small migrating birds, such as goldcrests, as well as by seabirds. Seals breed on the island, too.

▲ Goldcrest

LOCAL GOVERNMENT

UNITARY COUNCILS
East Lothian
Midlothian
West Lothian
City of Edinburgh

Note: pages 122–23 explain the different types of local authority and show the areas covered by the bodies in this region.

NORTH SEA

North Sea map showing Firth of Forth, Bass Rock, Edinburgh Airport, Edinburgh Castle, Edinburgh, North Berwick, Dunbar Castle, Dunbar, Almond, Water of Leith, Esk, Tyne, Pentland Hills, Moorfoot Hills.

▲ **Roofless ruins**
Linlithgow Palace, where Mary, Queen of Scots was born in 1542, was a favourite residence of Scottish kings. West Lothian used to be called Linlithgowshire.

LOTHIAN'S CASTLES

The region has several notable castles besides Edinburgh Castle. In 1339 the Countess of March and Dunbar, known as Black Agnes, successfully defended Dunbar Castle against a siege. Hailes Castle was reduced to ruins by Oliver Cromwell during the English Civil War. Crichton Castle was begun in the 1400s and enlarged in the 1500s. Tantallon Castle, which was owned by the Douglas family, is a cliff-top stronghold that juts into the North Sea.

▼ Black Agnes defends Dunbar

BRILLIANT BRIDGE

The Forth Rail Bridge was completed in 1890 after seven years' work and the loss of 60 workers' lives. The bridge's intricate, iron girders take three years to repaint. Nearby is the Forth Road Suspension Bridge, completed in 1964.

F

E

D

C

B

A

4   3   2   1

Clydeside

◀ **Bottlenose dolphin**
The Isle of Mull is a good place for spotting marine mammals such as minke whales, bottlenose dolphins and seals.

Coll

Tiree

Iona

▼ **Isle of Mull**
The tiny settlement of Calgary is built on a small, secluded bay on the northwest corner of the island.

THIS REGION EXTENDS FROM THE RIVER CLYDE in the south to Oban in the north. It was once part of the Kingdom of Strathclyde, which covered southwest Scotland and northwest England 1,000 years ago. Modern Strathclyde, which is Scotland's most densely-populated region, is dominated by the city of Glasgow.

In the northwest are sea lochs, peninsulas and islands, including part of the Inner Hebrides and the islands of Arran and Mull. The rest of the region is hilly and includes parts of the Central Lowlands, the Highlands to the north and the Southern Uplands to the south. The River Clyde flows through the Central Lowlands in a great curve, stretching for 170 kilometres from the Lowther Hills to Dumbarton. The Firth of Clyde completes the horseshoe shape.

◀ **Peregrine falcon**

Water world
Many of the lochs of Argyll and Bute are sea lochs or inlets, such as the Gare Loch and Lochs Long, Fyne, Goil, Gilp, Craignish and Melfort. Loch Linnhe in the north is the start of the Great Glen that crosses the Highland Region. Of the landlocked lochs, the largest are Loch Lomond, Loch Awe and Loch Etive. Fast-flowing mountains streams feed these lochs. 'Argyll' comes from the Gaelic *Earraghaidheal*, which means 'coastland of the Gael.'

▲ **Dunoon, Argyll**
This seaside resort is on the northwestern shore of the Firth of Clyde.

TLANT
OCEAN

Glasgow City
The Celtic for Glasgow, *Glas Ghu*, or the 'Green Glen,' refers to the valley where most of the city lies. The city straddles the River Clyde, with most business and industry on the north bank. Glasgow's heavy industries developed in the 1800s, but by the 1970s most had closed down. Today the city is a major trading and administrative centre. It has three universities, an airport and good transport links to England, Edinburgh and the north of Scotland. Glasgow has a busy port and the banks of the Clyde are lined with docks, quays and shipyards.

▼ **Sir Walter Scott**
Scott's statue looks out across the city of Glasgow from a 24-metre-high column in George Square.

▼ **Fingal's Cave**
This amazing cave on the uninhabited Isle of Staffa inspired composer Felix Mendelssohn to write his *Hebrides Overture*.

▶ Jet-skier

◀ Wild goat

LOCAL GOVERNMENT

UNITARY COUNCILS
Argyll and Bute
East Ayrshire
East Dunbartonshire
East Renfrewshire
Inverclyde
North Ayrshire
North Lanarkshire
Renfrewshire
South Ayrshire
South Lanarkshire
West Dunbartonshire
City of Glasgow

Note: pages 122–23 explain the different types of local authority and show the areas covered by the bodies in this region.

Mull

Dunstaffnage Castle

Oban

Orchy

Firth of Lorne

Jura

KILMARTIN VALLEY

Inverary Castle

Inverary

Lochgilphead

Argyll Forest Park

Loch Lomond

Dunoon

Gare Loch

Greenock

Dumbarton

Kirkintilloch

Sound of Jura

Bute

Glasgow Airport

Glasgow Cathedral

Glasgow

Motherwell

Paisley

Hamilton

Clyde

Lanark

KINTYRE

Arran

Ardrossan

Firth of Clyde

Irvine

Kilmarnock

LOWTHER HILLS

Campbeltown

Ayr

Doon

Mull of Kintyre

Girvan

Stinchar

NORTH CHANNEL

Ballantrae

LOCH LOMOND
This is the largest lake in Britain, with a maximum length of 36.4 kilometres and a surface area of 70 square kilometres. There are 37 islands in the loch, and it is a popular destination for watersports.

G

F

E

D

C

B

A

7   6   5   4   3   2   1

THERE WAS A PREHISTORIC SETTLEMENT on the site of modern Glasgow, but the city began to develop only after St Kentigern (also called St Mungo) founded a chapel there in AD543. He died at Glasgow. Argyll had been colonized by a Celtic people (known as Scots) from Ireland. The Scottish king, Kenneth MacAlpin, who ruled from 843 until 860, extended his rule over the Picts of northern Scotland. The southern part of the region formed the kingdom of Strathclyde, whose people were ancient Britons. Their king, Malcolm II, ruled from 997 until 1005 and was the first king of all Scotland.

▲ **Burns Monument**
This monument stands in Alloway, Ayrshire, which was the birthplace of Robert Burns. Scots celebrate the poet's birthday each January 25th (Burns Night), with feasting and poetry readings.

◄ **St Mungo's Museum**
Opened in 1993, St Mungo's Museum, Glasgow, has a collection of art related to world religions. There is a stunning Zen garden in the museum grounds.

▼ **Scottish heroine**
Flora MacDonald helped Bonnie Prince Charlie to escape Scotland after the Jacobite Rebellion in the 1700s. She disguised the Stuart prince as a maid for the journey. MacDonald's punishment was imprisonment in Dunstaffnage Castle on the shores of Loch Etive.

BRUCE AND THE SPIDER

Robert the Bruce freed Scotland from English rule and became king in 1306. At one stage in the war he was heavily defeated, and fled for safety to a cave on the Isle of Arran. He was in despair until he saw a spider try – and fail – to climb up its silk thread. The spider succeeded only on its seventh attempt. This inspired Bruce, and he went back to continue the fight. People thought this was just a legend until an arachnologist (a spider expert) examined the cave and found a species of spider that is famous for being a bad climber.

Castles

There has been a castle at Dumbarton since the 6th century, sited on a huge rock overlooking the river Clyde. Work on the castle at Rothesay, on the Isle of Bute, first began in the 1100s. The Vikings besieged the castle twice. The present building was largely rebuilt in the 1800s. Bothwell Castle was fought over by English and Scots, part of it being demolished in 1337.

◄ **Paisley patterns**
The town of Paisley, now in the suburbs of Glasgow, is famed for its patterned fabric. The swirling designs were copied from Indian Mughal art. Paisley became very popular in the 1960s.

▲ David Livingstone
This famous explorer and missionary was born in Blantyre, Lanarkshire, in 1813. The first European to visit central Africa, he named Victoria Falls after his queen.

▼ Campbell's castle
Archibald Campbell became Duke of Argyll in 1743. He rebuilt the family seat, Inverary Castle, and filled it with collections of books, porcelain and weaponry.

TOIL AND TROUBLE

One of Shakespeare's most famous tragedies is *Macbeth*. The 'Scottish play' tells how Macbeth, one of King Duncan's generals, kills Duncan to become king himself. Three witches that Macbeth met had foretold that he would be king. The real Macbeth died in 1057 and is said to lie buried on Iona.

Famous buildings

Inverary Castle, the seat of the Dukes of Argyll, is a large house that was built in the late 1700s. It was designed to look like a French château. Culzean Castle in Ayrshire, another big house, was designed by Robert Adam. Hill House at Helensburgh was designed by Charles Rennie Mackintosh in 1902. Glasgow Cathedral, which dates from 1200, contains the remains of St Kentigern, and is dedicated to him under his nickname of St Mungo.

DID YOU KNOW?

The clipper ship *Cutty Sark* was built at Dumbarton in 1869. It was named after a witch in Robert Burns' poem *Tam o' Shanter*, who wore a short shirt, or 'cutty sark.'

▼ Glasgow School of Art
This building was designed inside and out by the architect Charles Rennie Mackintosh in the 1890s. Mackintosh's functional, geometric style is known as Art Nouveau.

Industry

Glasgow and the towns near it along the River Clyde make up Scotland's industrial heartland. The industries located there include shipbuilding, aircraft construction, iron and steel manufacture, and a wide variety of light engineering, especially in the 'new towns' of Cumbernauld, East Kilbride and Irvine. There are whisky distilleries in the region, for example on the Hebridean islands of Islay and Jura.

▲ Ayrshire dairy cattle

Farming

Agriculture plays a small part in the economy of Strathclyde. Farmers raise cattle and sheep, and there is a flourishing line in market gardening.

Central Scotland

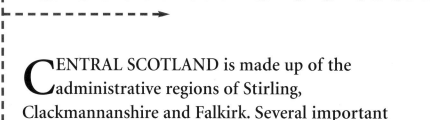

CENTRAL SCOTLAND is made up of the administrative regions of Stirling, Clackmannanshire and Falkirk. Several important battles between the Scots and the English took place in the area, including the Battle of Bannockburn in 1314.

Central Scotland lies between the Highlands and the Lowlands. In the north are seven mountains reaching to heights of 900 metres or more. The highest area in the south is the Campsie Fells, made up of extinct, eroded volcanoes. To the east of Loch Lomond, along the southern fringes of the Highlands, lies the scenic Queen Elizabeth Forest, which includes the peak of Ben Lomond and six picturesque lochs.

▼ Lomond's shore
Scotland's largest lake, Loch Lomond, forms the boundary between the Central and Strathclyde regions.

▲ Fruity folly
When this carved stone folly was built at Dunmore Park, Stirlingshire, in 1761, the pineapple was a rare luxury. Today, the building is let to holidaymakers.

Towns and buildings
The region's main settlement is Stirling, crisscrossed by the river Forth. Overlooking the river and the city centre, on a nearby hill, is the tower built as a national monument to the medieval Scottish hero Sir William Wallace. On another hill stands Stirling Castle, which was captured by Wallace in 1297. The castle has been altered many times since it was built in the 13th century. In the north of the region is Finlarig Castle, built by the Campbell clan.

▲ The Trossachs
Tourists are attracted to the rugged scenery of Central Scotland. The glen between Lochs Achray and Katrine is known as the Trossachs.

▼ The Battle of Bannockburn
In 1314 Robert the Bruce led a famous victory against the English at Bannockburn. This won Scotland's independence from England.

Industry and farming
Most of the region's industry is based in the south. Grangemouth, on the Firth of Forth near Falkirk, has a large oil refinery. Nearby factories produce a wide range of manufactured goods. Whisky distilling and brewing are also important in the area. Farmers in the north of the region rear sheep; in the south, where the soil is richer, crops are grown.

Moments in history

Stone Age people once lived on the banks of the River Forth. In AD141 the Romans built an earthworks across the region to mark the northern border of the Roman Empire. It was called the Antonine Wall, after Emperor Antoninus Pius, who ordered its construction. You can see remains of the wall near Falkirk.

Finlarig Castle

Queen Elizabeth Forest Park

▲ Ben Lomond

Teith

Forth

Stirling Castle

Stirling

Dunmore Park

Loch Lomond

CAMPSIE FELLS

Grangemouth

Falkirk

▲ Remains of the Antonine Wall

▲ Scottish thistle

◀ Wallace Monument, Stirling

▼ Castle Campbell
This castle near Dollar, Clackmannanshire, dates to the 1400s. It was nicknamed 'Castle Gloom.'

WILLIAM WALLACE

Sir William Wallace is one of Scotland's great heroes. In the late 1200s he led the fight for Scottish independence from England. In 1297 he scored a victory at Stirling Bridge, but he was defeated at Falkirk the following year and escaped to France. On his return to Scotland he was betrayed to the English, and was hung, drawn and quartered, without trial, for the crime of treason. A monument to Wallace was built at Stirling in the 1800s.

F

E

D

C

B

A

Along the Tay

▼ River Tay

▲ **Time for tee**
The rules of golf were first drawn up in the clubhouse at St Andrews in 1754.

T HE MIGHTY RIVER TAY, Scotland's longest river, dominates the region of Tayside and Fife. It flows through an area of rich, fertile farmland. The region includes the historic town of St Andrews, home to Scotland's oldest university (founded 1412) and the most famous golf course in the world.

The River Tay, which flows across the region and out into the sea in the Firth of Tay, contains more water than any other river in the British Isles. The north and west of Tayside are mountainous, with the Grampian Mountains in the northwest. The region has several large lakes, including Lochs Rannoch, Tummel, Tay and Leven. The land is flat and fertile in the south. Fife stretches out into the North Sea as a peninsula between the Firths of Tay and Forth.

Towns and industry

Dundee is the largest city in the region. It is an important engineering centre. Dundee is also famous for its marmalade and jam, but journalism is the biggest employer. Farther west, the city of Perth was capital of Scotland from AD836 to 1437. This is an important farming area, and cattle rearing is widespread. Soft fruits are grown in the area, which is known for its raspberries and tayberries. There is fishing on the south coast, with the port of Arbroath famed for its 'smokies' (smoked haddock).

▼ **Scone**
In AD838, Kenneth MacAlpin brought the Stone of Destiny to Scone, near Perth. Scottish kings were crowned on the Stone until the English carried it off in 1297.

▲ **Culross**
In the 1600s, the village of Culross was an important trade centre for salt and coal. Today, it is a perfectly-preserved Scottish burgh with beautiful, painted cottages.

Moments in history

In the Middle Ages, Scotland's parliament met at Perth, which was the home of Scottish kings. During the English Civil War this area was involved in some heavy fighting. Fife became known as a kingdom because it was a separate, Pictish province. As recently as 1975, local people argued hard to keep Fife's own identity.

▶ **Killiecrankie Pass**
This stunning gorge is just north of Pitlochry. At the spot called 'Soldiers' Leap,' Bonnie Dundee's Highland soldiers jumped across the Pass in 1689.

Castles

There are notable castles at Ravenscraig, St Andrews and Claypotts, where the castle is Z-shaped. Mary, Queen of Scots escaped from imprisonment in Loch Leven Castle. Princess Margaret was born at Glamis Castle, Angus, which was the childhood home of Queen Elizabeth, the Queen Mother. The Scottish king Macbeth is said to have lived in an earlier castle at Glamis in the 11th century.

LOCAL GOVERNMENT

UNITARY COUNCILS
Angus
Fife
Perth & Kinross
City of Dundee

Note: pages 122–23 explain the different types of local authority and show the areas covered by the bodies in this region.

▶ **Glamis Castle**
There has been a castle at Glamis for at least a thousand years. The present castle, built in the style of a French château, dates mainly from the late 17th century.

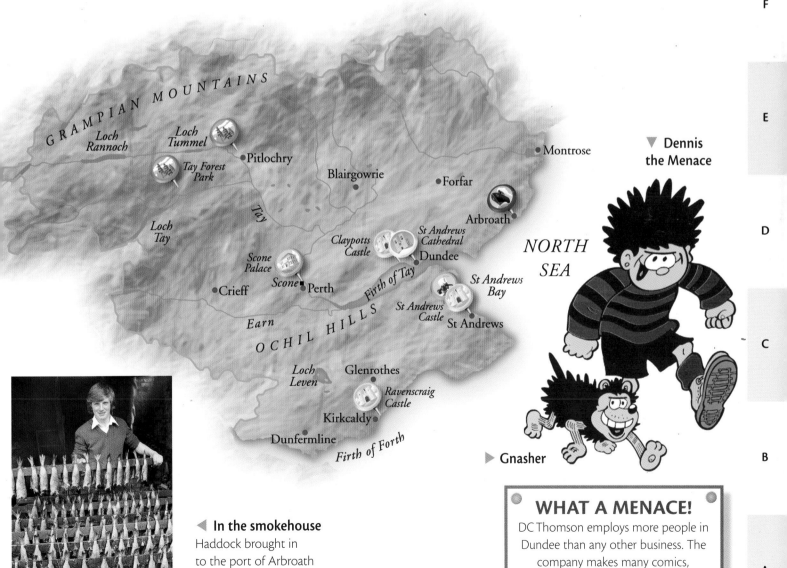

◀ **In the smokehouse**
Haddock brought in to the port of Arbroath are cured to make the town's famous 'smokies.'

▼ **Dennis the Menace**

▶ **Gnasher**

WHAT A MENACE!
DC Thomson employs more people in Dundee than any other business. The company makes many comics, including the world-famous *Beano*.

Northeast Scotland

T HE NORTHEAST CORNER OF SCOTLAND includes the former counties of Aberdeenshire, Banffshire, Kincardineshire and most of Morayshire. On the east coast of this mountainous region lies the port of Aberdeen, Scotland's third-largest city and centre of the Scottish oil industry.

The landscape of the region is dominated by the rugged Grampian Mountains. Several major rivers cut through this range, including tributaries of the River Spey which, at 172 kilometres long, is second only to the Tay in length and volume of water. Other rivers include the Deveron, Ythan, Don and Dee. The climate of this large region tends to be cool and windy, and snow lies on the mountains for much of the winter. The mountains shelter the rest of the region from the prevailing westerly rain-bearing winds.

Industry

Industry is mostly in the university city of Aberdeen, which lies at the mouth of the River Dee. The city was a bustling port as long ago as Viking times; today, it still has trade links with Scandinavia and the Baltic. Most importantly, though, it is a base for supplying and servicing oil platforms and drilling rigs in the North Sea. Aberdeen, Peterhead (another North-Sea oil centre), Buckie and Fraserburgh are key centres of Scotland's fishing industry. Whisky is distilled in the region, too. The town of Dufftown has seven working distilleries, including the famous Glenfiddich Distillery.

Farming

This is Scotland's leading farming region, producing barley, oats and wheat. Aberdeen Angus cattle are bred here. There are around 1,000 square kilometres of managed forests.

▼ **Speedy Spey**
Well-known for its salmon fishing, the Spey is also the fastest-flowing river in the British Isles.

▼ **Bred for beef**
The long coat of the Aberdeen Angus protects it from the harsh Scottish winters.

▲ **Granite city**
Robert the Bruce rewarded Aberdeen's loyalty with a Common Good Fund. To this day, money from the fund is spent on beautifying the grey-granite city with dazzling flower displays.

▼ **Tug-o'-war**
Near to the Queen's holiday residence, Balmoral, is the village of Braemar. The Highland Games are held at Braemar every August.

▲ **The oil industry**
Since the oil boom of the 1970s and 1980s, offshore oil rigs have drilled the North Sea for precious supplies of oil.

Moments in history

There are remains of Stone Age and Iron Age peoples across the region, including stone circles and hill forts. The region was part of the ancient Pictish kingdom. Celtic missionaries founded monasteries in the area in the 1st millennium AD. Among them was St Machar, an Irish-born bishop who founded the first church in what later became Aberdeen. The present-day twin-towered cathedral of St Machar stands on the site.

LOCAL GOVERNMENT

UNITARY COUNCILS
Aberdeenshire
Moray
City of Aberdeen

Note: pages 122–23 explain the different types of local authority and show the areas covered by the bodies in this region.

NORTH SEA

Buckie

Elgin

Banff

Deveron

Spey

Keith

Turriff

Kinnairds Head

Fraserburgh

Peterhead

Ythan

Inverurie

Don

Aberdeen Airport

Aberdeen Cathedral

Craigievar Castle

Aberdeen

Balmoral Castle

Ballater

Dee

CAIRNGORM MOUNTAINS

Braemar

GRAMPIAN MOUNTAINS

Dunnottar Castle

Stonehaven

CASTLES

BALMORAL CASTLE, ABERDEENSHIRE
Rebuilt during the 1800s, this is a private house belonging to the Queen.

CRAIGIEVAR CASTLE, ABERDEENSHIRE
This tall, graceful castle has fairytale towers and turrets of pink granite.

DUNNOTTAR CASTLE, ABERDEENSHIRE
Dunnottar stands on the cliffs near Stonehaven. The Scottish crown and sceptre (known as the 'Honours of Scotland') were hidden here during the English Civil War.

HUNTLY CASTLE, ABERDEENSHIRE
This ruined castle was once home to the Gordon clan. Above the doorway is a carving showing Christ, St Michael and the royal coat of arms.

▼ **Balmoral castle**

▲ **Barrels of whisky**
The Glenfiddich Distillery produces millions of bottles of single-malt whisky each year. The spirit, made from fermented barley, is aged in oak casks. These are handmade by Glenfiddich's own coopers (barrel-makers).

The Highlands

▼ **Ben Nevis**
At 1,343 metres, this is the highest peak in the whole British Isles.

THE SCOTTISH HIGHLANDS reach the northernmost tip of the Scottish mainland at John o'Groats. Although they cover a vast area, there are only eight people per square kilometre. This is a region of great beauty, with deep glens, rugged mountains and wild moors.

▲ **Glencoe**
This monument marks the events of February 13, 1692. Soldiers from the Campbell clan were staying with the MacDonalds at Glencoe. They slaughtered 38 of their hosts, on the orders of William III.

Most of the region is mountainous, but there are lowland areas along the north and east coasts and on the Isle of Skye to the west. The mainland part of the region is split by the Great Glen (Glen Mor), a huge fault valley which runs from southwest to northeast. The valley contains a chain of lakes, from the sea loch of Loch Linnhe in the south, continuing with Lochs Lochy, Oich and Ness, and ending at the Moray Firth. The artificial Caledonian Canal links these lochs. Dozens of other lochs are strewn across the region, many of which open directly to the sea.

▼ **Caithness glass**
The glass-blowing factory at Thurso makes beautiful paper-weights and vases.

Industry and farming

The region has no major cities: the largest place is the market town of Inverness. The most important industry is manufacturing equipment for the North Sea oil fields. There are aluminium smelters near Fort William and Kinlochleven, and textile mills and whisky distilleries. Apart from sheep-rearing on the hills, there is only limited farming. Large herds of wild deer are culled to provide venison, while fish farms produce salmon.

▼ **Monster of the deep**
Loch Ness is home to a legendary monster, 'Nessie'. Eyewitnesses describe a creature that looks like a prehistoric plesiosaur.

Moments in history

Around the AD500s the west coast of this region was colonized by Scots from Ireland. Later, Vikings settled in the coastal areas. From about AD1000 Highlanders were organized into clans – families sharing common descent. Sometimes, clan warfare broke out. The last battle on British soil took place in the Highlands in 1746 – the Battle of Culloden.

◄ **Plesiosaur**

Portree •

Skye

CUIL
HIL

Canna

Rhum

Eigg

► **Dunvegan Castle**
Home to the chief clan of Skye, the MacLeods, Dunvegan Castle dates to the 9th century.

Pentland Firth

John o'Groats

Thurso

CAITHNESS

Noss Head

Wick

Cape Wrath

Scottish wildcat

Point of Stoer

NORTH MINCH

Unapool

Lochinver

Helmsdale

Brora

Loch Ewe

Ullapool

Bonar Bridge

Tarbat Ness

BONNIE PRINCE CHARLIE

In 1745 Prince Charles Edward Stuart ('Bonnie Prince Charlie') led a rebellion against rule by George II. He wanted to restore the Stuart dynasty to the throne. Many Highlanders came to fight for him, but he was defeated at Culloden Moor in 1746. The Highlanders helped him flee to France.

Moray Firth

NORTH WEST HIGHLANDS

Dingwall

Nairn

Inverness *CULLODEN MOOR*

Stromeferry

Kyle of Lochalsh

Spey

Loch Ness

Findhorn

Aviemore

GLEN MÒR

Glen More Forest Park

Caledonian Canal

Ben Macdui ▲

Kingussie

CAIRNGORM MOUNTAINS

Loch Oich

▲ **Red squirrel**

Mallaig

Loch Lochy

Gulvain

Inverlochy Castle

Fort William

▲ *Ben Nevis*

Loch Linnhe

Kinlochleven

Glencoe

LOCAL GOVERNMENT

UNITARY COUNCIL
Highland

Note: pages 122–23 explain the different types of local authority and show the areas covered by the bodies in this region.

The Outer Hebrides

⬅ ···

THE OUTER HEBRIDES are a group of islands off the northwest coast of Scotland. They are also known as the Western Isles or Eilean Siar. Many of the islands are very small and are uninhabited. The largest island is Lewis with Harris (Lewis is the northern part). Regular ferries link the islanders with mainland Scotland. Many inhabitants still speak Scottish Gaelic as their first language.

To the south of Lewis with Harris are the three islands of North Uist, Benbecula and South Uist, which are linked by bridges. Farther south are Eriskay and Barra, which are reached by a ferry service. There are several smaller islands, including the uninhabited St Kilda group, 64 kilometres to the west. The Outer Hebrides are mostly mountainous, with large areas of open moorland and rolling, grassy plains. Sea lochs indent the craggy coastline, and there are hundreds of small, freshwater lochs inland. A range of hills divides Lewis from Harris, which ends in a long peninsula. The two are connected by a strip of land with a sea loch on either side.

Industry and farming

The chief industry of the islands is the production of Harris tweed. Some is manufactured in mills at Stornoway, the chief town, but most is made in the homes of local crofters. There are 5,500 crofts (smallholdings) on the islands, where sheep and cattle are raised and potatoes are grown. Yet less than six percent of the land is suitable for farming. Fishing fleets catch shellfish and a few herrings and whitefish. Tourism and fish farming, mainly of salmon, are growing industries.

▼ Celtic cross
There are 54 prehistoric standing stones at Callanish, Lewis. The stones are arranged in the shape of a cross.

▼ Whalebones
At Bragar, on Lewis, two whalebones form an arch by the side of the road. Hanging from the top of the arch is the harpoon used to kill the whale.

▲ Black house
At Eochar, South Uist, you can still find some thatched 'black houses.' Crofters lived in these Viking-style longhouses until the 1930s. Each turf-built house had a central, peat-burning fire but no chimney.

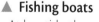

▲ Fishing boats
At low tide, the islanders' fishing boats are beached on the Island of Lewis.

◀ Bleak and black
The landscape of Lewis is dominated by the Black Moor. This peaty moorland is scattered with many tiny lochs.

Moments in history

There are several stone circles in the Western Isles, including Callanish which was begun 4,000 years ago. It is the largest prehistoric monument on the islands and has a central burial chamber. In the 9th century Vikings settled the islands, which were claimed by Norway until 1266. Three clans ruled the islands until after the Jacobite rising of 1745, when they came under the control of the United Kingdom government. Overpopulation and poverty caused many islanders to emigrate to America and Australia in the 1800s.

▼ **Seilebost, Island of Harris**
Tourists are attracted to the islands' stunning white-sand beaches, which rival any in the Caribbean.

ATLANTIC OCEAN

Butt of Lewis

Callanish •
Stornoway •
Eye Peninsula

Lewis

North Minch

ST KILDA

Harris

LOCAL GOVERNMENT

UNITARY COUNCIL

The Western Isles (Eilean Siar)

Note: pages 122–23 explain the different types of local authority and show the areas covered by the bodies in this region.

North Uist

Little Minch

Benbecula

South Uist

▼ **Harris tweed**

Kisimul Castle
Barra

SEA OF THE HEBRIDES

GIFT TO A GOD

During the 1600s, islanders on Lewis made sure to perform this special rite on October 31st each year. Someone would wade into the sea, chanting to call up the sea god, Shony. They offered the god a cup of ale in the hope of a good crop of seaweed. They used seaweed to fertilize their fields.

H

G

E

D

C

B

A

7   6   5   4   3   2   1   31

Orkney

▼ **Prepare to dive**
Scapa Flow is Europe's best diving site. Wrecks in the clear waters include three German battleships, sunk during World War I, and HMS *Royal Oak*, sunk during World War II.

THE ORKNEY ISLANDS LIE TEN KILOMETRES from the northeastern tip of mainland Scotland. The Orkney chain contains about 90 islands – as well as numerous holms (islets) and skerries (rocky reefs) – but only 21 of the islands are inhabited. Together with the Shetland Islands, the Orkneys make up the boundary between the North Sea and the Atlantic Ocean.

The Orkneys are separated from Scotland's north coast by a narrow channel called the Pentland Firth. There are steep cliffs on the west and south coasts of the islands, while the north and east coasts are jagged. Inland, the landscape is mostly low-lying, with rocks, swamps and small lochs. Much of the ground is peat-based, but there is some rich arable land. The climate is mild, with plenty of rainfall.

Important places

The largest island, Mainland, has two towns: Kirkwall, the capital, and the port of Stromness. The second-largest island is Hoy, which is part of a group called the South Isles. Off its rugged cliffs stands a detached rocky pillar known as the Old Man of Hoy. To the south, the islands of Burray and South Ronaldsay are linked to Mainland by causeways known as the Churchill Barriers. They were built during World War II to protect the waters of Scapa Flow, which were used by the Royal Navy.

▲ **Bird-watchers' paradise**
Steep cliffs on the tiny island of Copinsay provide nesting nooks for many types of seabird, including guillemots (*above*) and kittiwakes.

◄ **Old Man of Hoy**
This spectacular rock stack towers up to a height of 137 metres.

▼ **Prehistoric grave**
Built around 2750BC, Maes Howe was designed so the Sun's rays shone into the central chamber at the winter solstice. Vikings plundered the site and you can still see their runic graffiti on the chamber walls!

▼ **Ring of Brodgar**
This 91-metre-wide circle of standing stones was erected on Mainland during the Bronze Age. Thirty-six of the original 60 stones reach skywards to this day.

Industry and farming

Fishing, farming and craft industries are the main occupations of the Orkneys. The chief agricultural products are beef, dairy products, eggs and barley. Barley is malted at the Highland Park Distillery, Kirkwall, to make single-malt whisky. There is a North-Sea oil terminal on the island of Flotta. Air and sea services link the islands, and connect them with Shetland and the mainland of Scotland.

▲ **School air-bus**
Kirkwall airport operates a daily link to the Scottish mainland. Orcadian children have to take the plane to and from school!

Moments in history

Stone Age and Bronze Age peoples lived in Orkney, and they have left behind stone circles, underground houses and standing stones. The Romans knew the islands as the Orcades. Denmark owned the Orkney Islands from the AD800s until 1472. In that year the Scottish king, James III, married a Danish princess and the islands, along with the Shetlands, formed part of her marriage dowry.

Westray
North Ronaldsay
Sanday
Rousay
Stronsay
Mainland
Skara Brae ■
Kirkwall Cathedral
Shapinsay
●Kirkwall
Stromness●
NORTH SEA
Scapa Flow
Hoy
South Ronaldsay
Pentland Firth

LOCAL GOVERNMENT

UNITARY COUNCIL
Orkney Islands

Note: pages 122–23 explain the different types of local authority and show the areas covered by the bodies in this region.

SKARA BRAE

Skara Brae is a 5,000-year-old village on Mainland. It was preserved under sand from 2500BC, until a storm revealed it again in 1851. The walls of the huts – and the furniture, too – were built of stone slabs, because the Orkneys have few trees. By examining the remains, experts now know that the villagers grew barley and wheat, and raised cattle and sheep. They also caught seafood and hunted wild game.

▲ **Leatherback turtles**

F

E

D

C

B

A

5 4 3 2 1

Shetland Islands

▼ **Shetland pony**
The world's smallest breed of horse, the Shetland pony, is just over a metre tall.

▼ **Muckle Flugga lighthouse, Unst**
David Stevenson built Britain's most northerly lighthouse in 1854. His nephew, author Robert Louis Stevenson, stayed here to write his famous novel *Treasure Island*.

THE SHETLAND ISLANDS (also known as Zetland) are the most northerly of the British Isles. They lie 80 kilometres northeast of Orkney, and nearly 200 kilometres off the Scottish mainland. The nearest mainland town is Bergen, in Norway.

There are about 100 islands and islets, but less than 20 of them are inhabited. The largest island is Mainland, where more than half the people live. The other large islands are Yell, Unst, Feltar, Whalsay and Bressay. Fair Isle lies 40 kilometres south of the main group. Only about 100 people live there. Shetland is bleak, consisting mostly of moorland with few trees. The coasts are rocky, and are broken up by long sea lochs called 'voes.' The highest point is Ronas Hill (450 metres) on Mainland. The climate is humid and fairly mild, but the weather is always windy and there are often gales.

▼ **Sullom Voe**
This massive oil terminal is Europe's biggest. Two 160-km-long underwater pipelines carry crude oil there from the North-Sea oilfields.

Industry
North Sea oil has brought much-needed work to the Shetlanders. There is a huge oil terminal at Sullom Voe. Sumburgh Airport, on the southern tip of Mainland, operates a helicopter service out to the oil rigs, as well as services to the mainland cities of Aberdeen and Inverness.

▼ **Ness Yole**
This boat used for inshore fishing shows the influence of the Vikings, or Norsemen. Shetland was part of Norway from the 800s to the 1400s.

▼ **Fair Isle tank top**
An authentic Fair Isle knit must have been made on Fair Isle itself and have the distinctive OXOXO patterning.

Farming
Agriculture in Shetland is limited because of poor soil and rugged land. Most farmers work on crofts (smallholdings) and rear sheep. Shetland sheep produce fine-quality wool which is hand-knitted by the islanders. Hardy Shetland ponies are reared on Unst and some of the other islands. Fishing boats bring in catches of herring and whitefish to the ports of Lerwick and Scalloway. Fish farming is a growing industry.

Herma Ness

Unst

Yell

Fetlar

Scatsta Airport

•Sullom Voe

St Magnus Bay

Papa Stour

Whalsay

Mainland

NORTH SEA

Lerwick Castle

•Lerwick

Foula

Fair Isle

Moments in history

The earliest inhabitants of the Shetland Islands were prehistoric, and they have left behind many remains, including stone circles. The site of Jarlshof, in the south of Mainland, shows signs of continuous settlement over several centuries. There is a group of Bronze Age houses which were built in the 700s BC. Viking settlers arrived in the 8th century AD, and most Shetlanders today are of Norse descent. The islands belonged to Norway until 1472, when they were annexed to Scotland along with the Orkneys.

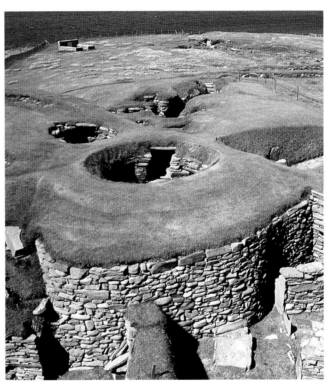

▲ **Jarlshof**
This prehistoric and Viking settlement was uncovered by a gale in the early 1900s.

▼**Up-Helly-Aa**

FESTIVAL OF FIRE

On the last Tuesday of January each year, Shetlanders remember their Norse past by celebrating the festival of Up-Helly-Aa. Groups of men dress up as Vikings and parade through the streets of Lerwick. They pull a specially-built Viking galley, with a carved dragon prow, down to the water's edge. There it is launched and set on fire. In Viking times, the bodies of dead chiefs were pushed out to sea in blazing longboats.

Glossary

Act of Union A law passed in parliament to join two (or more) countries together.

Anglo Saxon Relating to the Germanic peoples (including Angles, Saxons and Jutes) who settled England and Scotland.

arable Describes land used for growing crops rather than, for example, raising cows or sheep.

basalt A type of very hard, dark-coloured igneous rock.

Bronze Age The prehistoric time after the Stone Age, lasting from around 2300BC until 700BC, when people used bronze for tools and weapons.

devolution A type of home rule, where some parts of government are controlled locally instead of by the national parliament.

canal A man-made river, usually almost perfectly flat, that can be used to transport goods by boat.

causeway A raised road or pathway, for example over marshy land, or across a stretch of sea.

Celt A member of one of the prehistoric tribes of farmers that settled Britain and Ireland during the Iron Age. Celtic languages, such as Gaelic, are still alive today in Ireland, Wales, the Scottish Highlands and the Isle of Man.

clan Like a tribe, a group of people led by a single chieftain, especially in the Scottish Highlands. Clan members are often related and share the same surname.

climate The average weather of a place throughout the year.

continental drift The gradual movement of the Earth's land masses that breaks up existing continents and forms new ones.

crannog Gaelic word describing an artifical island on which a dwelling or fort has been built.

croft A smallholding, usually consisting of a tiny farm with a cottage.

cromlech A prehistoric stone structure, such as a tomb or standing stones.

dale Low-lying ground between hills; often, this is a river valley.

dam A large wall or bank built to hold back river water and raise its level.

distilling Process of purifying an alcoholic drink, such as whisky, by evaporating and condensing it.

dolmen A prehistoric stone structure, probably used as a tomb. It usually consisted of several standing stones with a flat stone placed on top.

earthwork A mound of earth used in prehistoric times as a fort.

erode To wear away the land. Wind, moving water and glaciers all erode the land.

escarpment The steep side of a hill, cliff or rock.

estuary The part of a river where it reaches the sea and often has tides; the river's mouth.

fault A crack in the rocks that form the Earth's crust. Fault lines are likely spots for earthquakes or volcanoes.

fell A hill, usually of uncultivated land such as pasture or moor.

firth The mouth of a river or an arm of the sea.

fishery A place where fish are caught.

flax Fibres from the *Linum* plant, used to make linen.

game Wild animals killed for food or sport, such as deer (for venison meat), geese or rabbits.

gasfield An area that has deposits of natural gas.

glacier A large sheet of ice, or ice and rock, that flows slowly down a valley like a frozen river.

glen A narrow, often wooded, valley.

gorge A deep, narrow canyon that cuts through the land.

granite A type of very hard, speckled igneous rock.

grove A small area of woodland.

Gulf Stream Warm water current that originates in the Gulf of Mexico and flows across the Atlantic to northwestern Europe.

headland A point of land that juts out into the sea.

hill fort A prehistoric stronghold on top of a hill.

home rule Self-government, as opposed to rule by another country.

hummock A small hill.

hydroelectric power Energy made by harnessing the movement of water, either downhill or in tides or waves.

igneous Describes a rock formed when volcanic lava cooled. Granite and basalt are both igneous rocks.

Industrial Revolution Period when the first factories were built. Instead of human labour, newly-invented, steam-powered machines performed repetitive or heavy tasks. In Britain, this began in the 1760s.

Iron Age The prehistoric time after the Bronze Age, beginning around 700BC, when people used iron tools and weapons.

inlet A small bay in a coastline.

islet A tiny island.

kirk A Scottish word for 'church.'

limestone A type of easily-eroded rock, such as chalk, that formed millions of years ago from the crushed shells and skeletons of tiny sea creatures.

loch Pronounced 'lock'. A Gaelic word meaning 'lake.' A loch may contain fresh or salt water.

managed forest Trees planted rather like a crop to be harvested for their timber. Felled trees are replaced with new saplings.

marina A harbour or dock where yachts are berthed.

market garden A garden where fruit, vegetables and flowers are grown for sale to the public.

medieval From the Middle Ages.

Middle Ages The time between the end of the Roman empire in the AD400s, until the explosion of invention and learning in the 1400s, known as the Renaissance.

mint A place where money is printed or coined.

monarch A head of state, for example a king or queen, who inherits their title.

moorland An expanse of wild, uncultivated land, which often has poor, peaty soil.

motte-and-bailey castle A type of castle built by the Normans, where the tower, or keep, is built on an earth mound (motte), surrounded by a walled courtyard (bailey).

national assembly An assembly of elected representatives that governs a country, or aspects of a country.

oil platform A steel or concrete structure that supports an oil rig out at sea. Some platforms are free-floating; others are fixed to the seabed.

oil rig The machinery and structures used to drill for oil.

outcrop Rock that is visible at the surface, rather than hidden under the soil.

paramilitary Describes a rebel group that is organized like an army.

parliament The seat of government. Some members of parliament are elected by the people (in Britain, they attend the House of Commons; in the Republic of Ireland, they attend the Dáil); others are born or appointed to a position in the upper house (in Britain, this is the House of Lords; in the Republic of Ireland, this is the Senate).

patron saint A saint considered to be protector of a country.

peat bog Marshy land where peat has formed. Peat is long-decayed vegetation, the first step in the process that produces coal.

pele tower A simple, fortified house, often entered by means of a ladder to the first floor.

Pict A prehistoric Celtic people that inhabited northeastern Scotland.

plain An area of flat or gently-undulating land, usually low-lying.

plantation of Ireland The settling of Ireland from the 1600s by English and Scottish people, so Britain could establish control.

plateau An area of level, high ground.

plug Rock that has hardened inside a volcano's central hole, or vent.

pothole A deep hole eroded in limestone.

prehistoric From the time before there were any written historical records.

prevailing wind The wind that blows most often in a particular place or region.

principality A territory ruled by a prince or princes.

Protestant Church A branch of Christianity that has separated from the Roman Catholic Church. Protestant churches first formed during the Reformation.

province A distinct part of a country, treated differently to the rest of the country.

reef A chain of underwater rocks, usually closer to the surface than the surrounding seabed.

refinery A place where raw ingredients are processed, for example an oil or sugar refinery.

regeneration The creation of new buildings and businesses in a place.

republic A country without a monarch as head of state, that is governed entirely by elected representatives of the people.

Roman Catholic Church The first Christian Church, headed by the Pope in Rome. Catholic means 'universal.'

rune A symbol that is a character, or letter, from one of the alphabets used by Germanic peoples between the 3rd and 13th centuries.

slate Shiny, green- or blue-grey rock made up of thin plates, often used for roofing tiles.

smallholding A small plot of land, usually used for farming.

smokehouse A place where meat, fish or cheese is smoked, usually over a wood fire.

solar power Energy from the Sun.

solstice The day that the Sun is farthest away from the Equator. This happens twice in a year on the longest and shortest days, June 21st and December 21st.

stack An isolated pillar of rock, usually poking out of the sea.

standing stone A huge stone set upright in the ground. They were erected by prehistoric peoples, probably for religious purposes.

Stone Age The prehistoric time before the Bronze Age, from around 4000BC until 2300BC, when people used tools and weapons made of stone, such as flint. The period is split into the Old Stone Age (Paleolithic) and New Stone Age (Neolithic).

stone circle A ring of prehistoric standing stones.

supertanker A huge boat that carries a liquid cargo, such as oil.

suspension bridge A bridge with its deck supported from above by large cables or chains hanging from towers.

tributary A stream or river that flows into – and becomes part of – another, larger river.

tweed Rough, woollen cloth. Much of it is produced in the valley of the river Tweed.

Viking A Scandinavian people who invaded or raided parts of Britain between the AD700s and 1000s.

volcano A vent in the Earth's crust, out of which molten rock, ashes and steam erupt.

wetland Marshy land.

wold A low hill.

MAP CO-ORDINATES

Co-ordinates provide a way to find a place on a map. On each map page there is a border at the bottom that is divided into numbered blocks, and a border at the edge that is divided into lettered blocks. Together with the page number, these border numbers and letters are used to create the co-ordinates.

How do I give a place on a map its own co-ordinates?

1 Write down the page that the place is on. This is the first co-ordinate. If you want co-ordinates for Glasgow, then '19' is the first part, because Glasgow appears on the map on page 19.

2 Next put your finger on the place itself. Trace down to the bottom of the page and see which numbered block you reach. This number is the second co-ordinate. In the case of Glasgow, you reach number '4.'

3 Now put your finger back on the place and trace across to the edge of the page to see which lettered block you reach. This is the last co-ordinate. In the case of Glasgow, you reach letter 'D.'

4 Write down the three co-ordinates, separating them with commas so that they don't get muddled together. The co-ordinates for Glasgow would be '19, 4, D.'

Index

Numbers in *italics* refer to illustrations.

Acknowledgements

The publishers would like to thank the following artists whose work appears in this title:

Lisa Alderton/Advocate, Vanessa Card, Kuo Kang Chen; Wayne Ford, Terry Gabbey/AFA Ltd., Jeremy Gower, Ron Hayward, Gary Hincks, Sally Holmes, Richard Hook/Linden Artists, The Maltings, Janos Marffy, Terry Riley, Andrew Robinson, Peter Sarson, Mike Saunders, Christian Webb/Temple Rogers, Mike White/Temple Rogers, John Woodcock.

PHOTOGRAPHIC CREDITS

The publishers thank the following sources for the use of their photographs:

6 (B/L) Sant'Emidio, Ascoli Picena, Bridgeman Art Library; 7 (B/L) S.J.Taylor/Still Moving Picture Co.; 8 (T/R) Cairngorm Marketing; 10, (B/L) Doug Corrance/Still Moving Picture Co, (C/R) Ken Paterson/Still Moving Picture Co, (B/R) S.J.Taylor/Still Moving Picture Co;11 (C) S.J.Taylor/Still Moving Picture Co, (T/L)Skyscan;13 (B/L) Libby Withnall; (B/R) Macduff Everton/Corbis; 18 (B/R)Ian Britton, 20 (C/L) Glasgow Museums; 21 (B/L) Glasgow School of Art, (T/C); 23 (T/R) Falkirk Museum, (C/R) The National Wallace Monument; 25 (B/L) Angus Tourist Board, (B/R) D.C.Thomson & Co.Ltd; 27 (B/L) Glenfiddich Distillery; 28 (C/L) Caithness Glass Ltd., (C/R) West Highland Museum; 31 (B/L) Harris Tweed Assoc.; 32 all by Richard Welsby; 34 (C/R) British Petroleum Co., (B/L) Just Shetland, (T/L) Richard Welsby; 35 (B) Shetland Times;(C/R) Kevin Schafer/Corbis.

Every effort has been made to trace and credit all images used and the publishers apologise if any have been omitted.

All other photographs from MKP Archives.